Vanessa
the pig with the
wiggly waggly ears

Colin West

Hodder
Children's
Books

a division of Hodder Headline plc

Copyright © 1995 Colin West

First published in 1995 by Hodder Children's Books
A division of Hodder Headline plc
338 Euston Road
London NW1 3BH

The right of Colin West to be identified as the Author
of the Work has been asserted by him in
accordance with the Copyright, Design and Patents
Act 1988

2 4 6 8 9 7 5 3 1

ISBN 0340 62656 9

A catalogue record for this book is available
from the British Library.

Printed and bound in Great Britain
by Cox and Wyman Ltd, Reading, Berks.

Chapter One

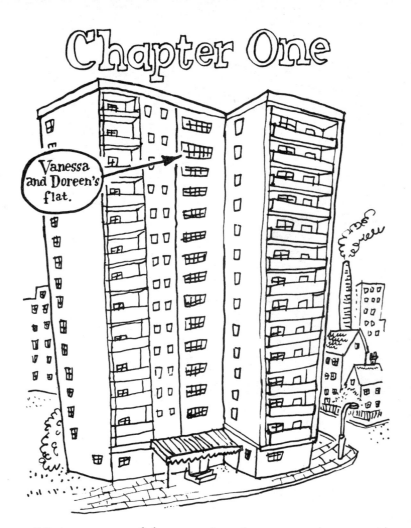

Vanessa and her twin sister
Doreen lived near the top of a
highrise flat in downtown
Grimsville.

Doreen, who was the eldest by
seventeen minutes, was a talented
singer, a gifted musician and an
accomplished tap dancer.

Doreen put on shows in which she entertained friends and relations. Everyone agreed she was almost good enough to go professional.

Vanessa could always be found sitting in the front row at these concerts. She was very proud of her talented sister.

"Doreen just needs a lucky break to make it really big," she thought. "I'll see if I can help out."

Vanessa invited the famous
talent spotter, Bernie Bartle, along
to one of Doreen's shows.

Mr Bartle sat through Doreen's
singing, dancing and musical turns
with his head in his hands. He
didn't look too happy.

"What's wrong?" Vanessa asked
afterwards. The impresario threw
his arms in the air.

I've seen twenty singers since Tuesday. I've seen six musicians this morning. And I've seen eighteen dancers since lunchtime. What I need is something DIFFERENT, something VIBRANT, something NEW!

Vanessa was sorry she'd wasted his time.

"There's just one thing," said Mr
Bartle, as he put on his coat.
"I couldn't help noticing that you
kept waggling your ears when
your sister was playing the
accordian."

"It's just a habit," said Vanessa.
"I always waggle my ears in time
with the music. I could always
stop, if it bothers you."

"No, don't do that!" said the
impresario hastily. "I like it.
There could be a future in it
for you."

11

"What do you mean?" asked
Vanessa, looking curious.
"Well, not many pigs can waggle
their ears like you," said Mr Bartle.
"Can I have another look?"

Feeling rather embarrassed,
Vanessa waggled her ears for
Mr Bartle.

She waggled
them up,

she waggled
them down,

she waggled
them left,

14

she waggled
them right,

she waggled
them backwards

and she waggled
them forwards.

The impresario was impressed.
"You could be the Next Big
Thing!" he said. "Just imagine,
your name in lights."

"You'll be a sensation!" he added.
"The biggest thing since sliced
bread!"

"Do you really think so?" asked
Vanessa, perking up. "I've never
thought of myself as a star. I
always thought Doreen was the
talented one."

"Trust me," said the impresario.
"It was me who discovered Maria
Schloss, remember."

Vanessa had never heard of Maria
Schloss, but she didn't like to
admit it.
"Is that so?" she murmured.
"Fancy that."

Chapter Two

That evening Vanessa sat down
to tell her sister about the
impresario's visit.

"Tell me," said Doreen excitedly, "which of my turns did he like the most? My singing, my dancing, or my accordian-playing?"

"He didn't like any of them," replied Vanessa bluntly. "He thinks *I'm* the talented one."

Doreen's mouth dropped.
"But what can you do?" she asked.
"This!" replied Vanessa, waggling
her ears left, right, up, down,
backwards and forwards.

Doreen was amazed.
"Ear waggling!" she screamed.
"What's so special about that?"
"Well, can you do it?" asked
Vanessa.

Doreen furrowed her brow.

She twitched her nose.

She crossed her eyes.

But for all her pulling and straining, she couldn't waggle her ears.

"Huh!" said Doreen snootily.
"Who wants to watch someone
waggling their ears anyway?"

"Plenty do! Mr Bartle says so,"
Vanessa replied. "He thinks I
could be the Next Big Thing!"

"We'll see who's the Next Big Thing!" said Doreen, sticking out her tongue.
Vanessa waggled her ears right back.

Chapter Three

Vanessa and Doreen planned a
concert. The biggest one yet.
They hired a local hall for the
evening and put ads in the papers
and posters up round town.

Before long everyone was
talking about the concert starring
the two duelling sisters.

When the day of the concert
arrived, there was a really good
turn out.

Mr Bartle was sitting in the front
row, waiting for Vanessa's ear
waggling act. He wanted to see
how it would go.

But first he had to sit through
Doreen's singing, playing and
dancing. The audience applauded
politely at the end of each piece,
but that was all.

Then it was Vanessa's turn.
She entered rather nervously and
stood in the spotlight.

The backing tape started and
Vanessa began waggling her ears
to the strains of the *William Tell
Overture.*

First she waggled her ears left
and then right.
The audience gasped.

Then she waggled her ears up and
then down.
The audience giggled.

Then she waggled her ears
backwards and then forwards.
The audience roared.

Vanessa waggled one ear up and
one ear down. Then she waggled
one ear left and one ear right.

She waggled her ears
independently and she waggled
her ears together.

The audience went wild.
They'd never seen anything like
Vanessa, the pig with the wiggly
waggly ears!

There was rapturous applause.
She had to take nineteen
curtain calls.

Vanessa finally came off stage and
Mr Bartle signed her up straight
away.

Chapter Four

News of Vanessa's act spread
like wildfire.
She gave concerts.
She gave interviews.

Theatres filled to overflowing.

Newspapers printed articles.

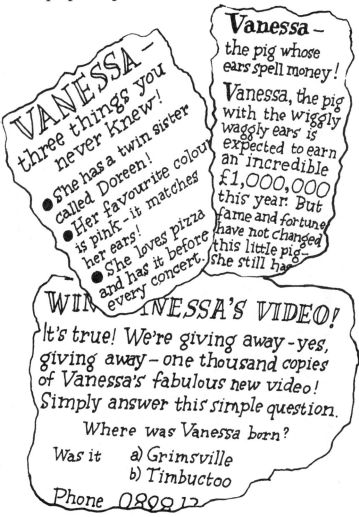

Vanessa – the pig whose ears spell money!

Vanessa, the pig with the wiggly waggly ears is expected to earn an incredible £1,000,000 this year. But fame and fortune have not changed this little pig – she still ha—

VANESSA – three things you never knew!

- She has a twin sister called Doreen!
- Her favourite colour is pink – it matches her ears!
- She loves pizza and has it before every concert.

WIN VANESSA'S VIDEO!

It's true! We're giving away – yes, giving away – one thousand copies of Vanessa's fabulous new video! Simply answer this simple question.

Where was Vanessa born?

Was it   a) Grimsville
         b) Timbuctoo

Phone 0899 12—

41

Soon Vanessa was on
breakfast TV.

Then she had her very own
Saturday night TV show.

She received over a thousand fan letters in a week.

Vanessa bathed in bubbles and had a pink Rolls Royce and a big mansion.

She had to hire a personal
secretary, a hairdresser and a
bodyguard.

Vanessa gave performances all
over the world. She was big in
Belgium, huge in Hawaii and
gigantic in Gibraltar.

Life was one long party and she
hardly ever thought of the old
days and of life back at Grimsville.

Chapter Five

One day Vanessa woke up in her hotel bed in Rio and went to the bathroom mirror to do her early morning ear exercises.

Her ears still ached from the
concert the previous night, which
had been a particularly trying one.

As she tried to do her warm-up
exercises, she was horrified to find
her ears didn't move.

Vanessa couldn't twitch either of
them the slightest bit. She was
dumbstruck. She sat down on the
bed and cried.

A doctor was called. He announced Vanessa's ears were suffering from nervous exhaustion from the constant waggling. They needed a good long rest.

Chapter Six

Vanessa had to cancel all her
future performances and retire to
a rest home.

She received piles of Get Well
cards, endless bouquets and
countless boxes of chocolates.

Amongst all the cards was a little
one with a picture of a spotlight
on the front. It was from her
sister Doreen.

Vanessa was reminded of the old times. She thought back to how life was before she was famous. In those days she could shop without being pestered.

She could eat out and not be bothered by autograph collectors.

And, above all, she could attend
her sister's concerts and waggle
her ears in time with the music.

Vanessa realised she preferred life in those days. She picked up the phone and dialled Doreen's number.

"Guess who?" she said excitedly.
"It's your sister Vanessa!"
She apologised for not keeping in touch, and told Doreen she had some important news.

"I'm retiring!" said Vanessa with a
whoop of delight. "I'm fed up
with show business."

"Are you mad?" screamed Doreen.
"You must be worth a million!"

"Seventeen million, actually," said
Vanessa. "I've got more than
enough money now, so I'm
retiring young and coming home
to Grimsville. We can set up
home in a nice part of town!"

Chapter Seven

Vanessa did just as she said. She
flew home after a good long rest
and returned to Grimsville.

Mr Bartle wasn't too pleased, but he wished Vanessa well in her retirement.

Lots of Vanessa's fans were
disappointed too, but they soon
got over it. They could still hire
the videos, after all.

Vanessa bought a nice house in
Crocus Lane, where she lived
happily with her sister.

Doreen still puts on concerts for her friends and relations. She still sings, dances and plays the accordion, and she's still nearly good enough to go professional.

And sitting in the back row,
(wearing dark glasses so no one
will recognise her) is always
Vanessa, quietly waggling her ears
in time with the music.